500 Writing Prompts
for Fiction, Journaling, Blogging and Creative Writing

By S. A. M. Richards

500 Writing Prompts

for Fiction, Journaling, Blogging and Creative Writing

"If you want to be a writer, you must do two things above all others: read a lot and write a lot." ~ Stephen King

Beat writer's block with 500 writing prompts and finish that novel, journal, poem, assignment, or blog post. Get your creative juices flowing and stretch your writing muscles with this fun collection of prompts.

This exciting resource of creative writing exercises is designed to help fiction writers and creative writing students crush their writer's block.

This book is designed to unlock a treasure trove of awesome ideas to start your own story, novel, poetic journal, blog post, or writing assignment.

Have fun with these prompts!

"If there's a book that you want to read, but it hasn't been written yet then you must write it."
— **Toni Morrison**

Dear Reader,

Welcome to *500 Writing Prompts for fiction, journaling, blogging, and creative writing.* I hope you find this collection helpful as a springboard to boost your imagination, spark your creativity and beat writer's block. This collection is useful for romance writers, mainstream fiction writers, non-fiction writers, college students, students in English classes, creative writing classes and for those who love poetic journaling of their day-to-day life.

So, what is writer's block? It's when your pen slowly slips through your fingertips, along with your ideas. Your mind suddenly draws a blank across the window of your thoughts. As if your ideas have cancelled out on you at the last minute—just packed up and left your mind without notice. Emptiness gladly overextends its stay. You must write that story, that poem, that novel, that blog post, or that article. So why is your pen not moving? Or why are the keys on your keyboard still? You must have something to say, but you just can't say it or write it. You may have writer's block. And this book will help you unlock the closed door to your ideas.

One of the easiest ways to do that is to keep the flow of your creative juices running by writing about anything that interests you, or any thought that slides into your mind.

Here are some rules that you'll find helpful when using this book. Remember, you can be flexible and do what works for you.

    1. Relax. It's important to not be critical. Just write what comes to mind. You can always make

changes later. The hardest part is usually getting started but this book will give you ideas.

2. Time yourself. You can give yourself 10 seconds or 10 minutes or more to write for each prompt.

3. Write every day, if possible. Even if you spare two minutes a day. That will make a difference and get you into the daily writing habit.

4. Have fun and look around you. This book is meant to spark your ideas and ideas are all around us.

Keep your eyes and your ears alert and soak in the beauty of your surroundings. You may set a timer to do the exercises in the book or you can write to your heart's content. It's totally up to you. Writers are as unique as their fingerprints. We're all different. Different styles and things work for different people. Be you.

You may use these prompts to boost your imagination to write fiction, essays, poetry, short stories, scenes for a play, a blog post or a journal entry.

May your ideas flow like the river of eternal stories.
S. A. M. Richards

Prompts 1 – 50

1. You've just won the grand prize in the lottery draw of $10,536,000. Congratulations! Describe how you feel. List ten things you would do with the money.

2. You've just been invited to the royal wedding. Describe what you will be wearing from head to toe. Have fun!

3. Your life is a Broadway stage play. What is the title of your play? Who are the main characters in your life? Is there someone you would re-cast?

4. You are walking through an enchanted forest. What do you see? What sounds do you hear?

5. You were asked out to a restaurant by your hot date and after dinner, your date surprises you by pulling out his calculator to add up what each of you will be paying for the dinner. Write how you feel about that?

6. If you could snap your fingers and become anyone in the world, who would that be?

7. If you could be anyone in history, who would it be and describe a typical day in your life as that historical figure.

8. You wake up one day and suddenly, you're the latest model of a smartphone. What's going through your mind? Describe a typical day with your user.

9. You're a time-travelling journalist and you've been sent back to 1899 and you have a chance to interview a prominent figure. What questions would you ask them?

10. Oops, you just sent a very personal email to the wrong recipient. Describe what you would do next in a dialogue with a friend.

11. Describe your perfect soul mate.

12. Create a list of your top 20 best traits. For example, your style, your upbeat personality, your talents…

13. If you carry a handbag, list the contents in your handbag and explain why you carry those items around with you. If you carry a wallet, list the contents in it.

14. List your ten favorite apps on your smartphone and explain why you love them.

15. You were supposed to buy a lottery ticket for a friend but you forgot. Now their winning numbers have come up. Write a dialogue about between the two friends.

16. Your character just got caught in a little white lie about why they took the day off work. Write a dialogue between your character and their boss.

17. Your friend has glossophobia (fear of public speaking) but has to give a speech in front of thousands of people. Describe how they are feeling. What advice would you give them?

18. You come home one evening to realize that
everything in your home has come alive, even
the furniture. Describe the scene.

19. List one superpower you wish you possessed.
Now, write a paragraph about how you would
use your new power. Who would you tell?
Would you keep it a secret?

20. Write a story about one of your ancestors.
Imagine what their typical day would be like.

21. Write a story about being able to read the mind
of the person standing next to you.

22. Write a story about a character in a chaotic job.

23. There are more pyramids in Sudan than in
Egypt. If you could travel back in time, what
would you say to those building the pyramids.

24. If you could come back in another life as
anything, what would you come back as, and
what would you do on your first day?

25. You're set up on a blind date by a friend. When you go to the restaurant, you're stunned to see your ex sitting there at your table. What would you say?

26. Write 10 affirmations on living a better life. You can start with "I am" or "I will" …

27. Write a poem about your favorite fruit. Remember to include the shape, the feel, the scent, the texture and the taste of it.

28. Finish the following sentence: I will never give up…

29. What is your favorite room in your home and why? Describe your room.

30. What is your earliest memory of your friends at school?

31. List five things that make you smile.

32. List your top ten favorite books to read or top 10 favorite games to play.

33. Who is your favorite celebrity and why?

34. Write a poem about the following words: I am
    enjoying life, one day at a time.

35. Write a paragraph about having fresh fruits and
    pancakes for breakfast.

36. Write a sentence that ends with the words
    "…and that's what I believe."

37. Describe the person staring back at you in the
    mirror. Use all five senses.

38. Write a story about the day in the life of a
    modern-day princess.

39. Write a story about the day in the life of your
    pet.

40. You just found out you have a genie within you.
    Which three wishes would you grant for
    yourself or for others?

41. Write a sentence about this news headline: Star Exposed

42. Write a letter beginning with "Dear Secret Santa"

43. Write a letter beginning with "Dear Secret Crush"

44. Use your five senses to describe an orange.

45. Finish this short letter: Dear Nosy Neighbor,

46. You've just booked your favorite vacation. Name 10 things you would pack with you.

47. Some people are a jack-of-all-trades. List 10 things you do well.

48. Write a story about a receptionist who overhears a plot.

49. Write a story about the many ways you recharge your spirit.

50. Write a story about a character hearing strange noises coming from the attic.

"The first draft is just you telling yourself the story."
– Terry Pratchett

Prompts 51-100

51. Write a story about a character making fun and outlandish New Year's resolutions.

52. Name 10 things you look for in a soul mate.

53. Name 7 ways you like to dress.

54. Name 5 people who are the closest people to you.

55. Name 3 people you could call at 4 am in the morning, if you needed to.

56. List four colors that remind you of the fall/autumn season.

57. What are your favorite colors?

58. Write a story about visiting a magical treehouse that comes alive.

59. Write a story about your dream job.

60. Write a funny letter about advice you would give to your younger self.

61. Write a story about a character's worst boss. Ever!

62. Write a story about a character who has the best boss. Ever!

63. Write a poem about what you enjoy about writing. How does it make you feel?

64. Make a list of the things you enjoy writing.

65. Build a fictitious town. What would you call it? What makes it so special?

66. Write a blog post about what you love about your home or your neighborhood.

67. Write a blog post about the places you love to shop.

68. Write a blog post about your favorite books.

69. Write a blog post about your favorite quotes.

70. Write a blog post about your top 10 lists of
things everyone should have.

71. Write a blog post about the many different ways
to save money or to earn money.

72. Write a poem about the different ways you relax
and unwind after a long day at work or school.

73. List 7 items you love to purchase.

74. Describe how you make your favorite dish or
meal.

75. Write about a cashier who has 100 customers in
line and no help in sight.

76. Write a story about showing up to the wrong
fitness class and not being able to leave.

77. Write a story about showing up to the wrong audition.

78. Write a story about a character being mistaken for a celebrity and being instantly showered with gifts and admiration.

79. Write a story about being stranded at the airport during a snowstorm or blizzard.

80. Write a funny story about two people who are totally opposite being stuck in the same room after being double-booked.

81. Write a story about visiting a nice ranch with horses.

82. Write a blog post about your favorite foods and tasty dishes.

83. Write a story about working undercover as a secret shopper.

84. Write a story about a librarian and a gamer stranded in a cabin.

85. Make a list of ten people you are grateful to have in your life.

86. List 10 things you are eternally grateful for.

87. List your top 10 favorite stores to shop.

88. Make a list of 10 people who fill your heart with joy.

89. Describe what you do in a typical day beginning with prying your eyes open in the morning.

90. Write a story about an overachiever and a laid-back person stranded in a cabin during a camping trip.

91. Write a short story about a neat freak and a messy person sharing an apartment for the month while housesitting for a mutual friend.

92. You just received an envelope with $50,000 in cash with a note saying the giver is just paying it forward after winning the lottery. What do you do next?

93. Invent a planet. What would you call it? What about the inhabitants? What makes this planet so special?

94. Write a story about a character curling up with a good book by the fireplace in the middle of a storm.

95. Write a story about a female tow truck driver who helps a male nanny with a broken-down car.

96. Write a story about an optimist and a pessimist having to plan a party together. What could they learn from each other?

97. You've just won a prize on a radio contest. You have just been credited with $100,000 in a gift card visa but there's a catch. You have to spend the money online in one hour. What would you buy? Which retail websites would you visit?

98. You just found out your pet is trending on social media because it has been discovered to have special powers and is the last of its kind. What do you do?

99. Describe a moment when you couldn't stop
    laughing.

100.   What is your earliest memory of going to
    school?

"Read a thousand books, and your words will flow like a river."— Lisa See

Prompts 101-150

101. List 5 things you are so thankful for.

102. List 5 areas in your life you are planning to improve.

103. List 5 different hair colors you would love to try.

104. List 5 things you do after you wake up in the morning.

105. List 5 foods you love to devour when you get the chance.

106. List 5 fruits that tantalize your taste buds.

107. Write a story about a chef whose kitchen appliances and spices come alive.

108. Write a list of rules for anyone entering your kitchen.

109. Write a story using the words "door," "cat," and "magic."

110. Write a conversation about asking your boss for a raise.

111. Write a conversation about talking someone down from a ledge.

112. Write a conversation about getting help with the housework.

113. Write a dialogue involving friends on the opposite side of an issue.

114. Write a dialogue about trying to book a much-needed vacation.

115. Write a story about a day in the life of a dog-walker.

116. Write a story about a person who accidentally mails a letter that no one was intended to see. The person makes attempts to retrieve it.

117.   Write a story about a person who accidentally sends a personal photo of themself to their contact list. What do they do next?

118.   Write a story about a person receiving a text message from a secret admirer.

119.   Write a story about a person taking a horseback riding lesson for the first time.

120.   Write a scene about someone waiting anxiously for a test result.

121.   Write a scene about someone looking everywhere for their cell phone.

122.   Write a scene about preparing for a snowstorm.

123.   Write a scene about a couple departing for their first enchanted cruise ship vacation.

124.   Write a story beginning with the quote "When you lose a false friend, you don't lose anything."

125.   Write a freestyle poem beginning with the line "You've got one chance to…"

126.   Write a poem about a beautiful sunset.

127.   Two people stumble upon a hidden treasure in their backyard. Write a dialogue between the two characters.

128.   Write a story using the words "magic," "candle," "cabin."

129.   You have 10 seconds to list any word that comes to your mind. Go!

130.   You have the magical ability to freeze time for 10 seconds. How would you use this newfound power? Give an example.

131.   Finish this sentence: You only live…

132.   Finish this sentence: I finally managed to…

133. Write a journal entry of your pet stuck inside on a snowy winter day.

134. Write a poem using the words "blueberries," and "enchanted forest."

135. Write a description of your favorite season.

136. Write the words that come to mind when you think of Summer.

137. Write the words that come to mind when you think of Fall or Autumn.

138. Write the words that come to mind when you think of Winter.

139. Write the words that come to mind when you think of Spring.

140. List 10 tips you would give for someone starting a new relationship.

141.   Make a list of fun things to do when stuck inside during a blizzard.

142.   Finish this sentence: He glowed…

143.   Write a paragraph starting with the sentence, "When I was younger…"

144.   Write a story about a calendar that is enchanted.

145.   Write a paragraph about the type of clothes you like to wear.

146.   Write a poem about the word "Charmed."

147.   What is your most comfortable outfit to wear?

148.   Using five senses, write a poem about the word "Peach."

149.   Write a short story using the words "feather," "door," and "cat."

150.   Write a story about the day in the life of a
        drama teacher.

"You can always edit a bad page.
You can't edit a blank page."
— Jodi Picoult

Prompts 151-200

151.   Write about a time you helped someone.

152.   Write about a time when you ate too much.

153.   Write about a time when you tried to lose weight.

154.   Write about a time when you reached out to someone.

155.   Write a dialogue between two people beginning with the words "How's it going?"

156.   Write a poem about the day in the life of a frog that used to be a prince.

157.   What is your earliest memory of you playing your favorite sport?

158.   Write a paragraph about the advice you would give to someone starting a new job they disliked.

159.   Write a story beginning with the sentence "Life is an adventure."

160.   Write a story about the quote by Confucius "Everything has beauty, but not everyone sees it."

161.   Write a story based on the Confucius quote "Wherever you go, go with all your heart."

162.   Write a poem about the Confucius quote "Your life is what your thoughts make it."

163.   Write a story about a superstitious man who refuses to step on cracks on the sidewalk or walk under a ladder.

164.   Write a paragraph about the African proverb "Knowledge is a garden. If it isn't cultivated, you can't harvest it."

165.   Write a story about the African proverb "Tomorrow belongs to people who prepare for it today."

166.   Write a story about the African proverb "Don't think there are no crocodiles just because the water is calm."

167.   Write a paragraph beginning with "Love is a painkiller."

168.   Write a paragraph beginning with the proverb "To get lost is to learn the way."

169.   Write a dialogue between two people with one asking the other for forgiveness.

170.   Write a story in the setting of an earthquake.

171.   Write a story set on a cruise ship.

172.   Write a story set inside a wedding ceremony.

173.   Write a story set in the 1980s.

174.   Write a story set in the year 1800.

175.   Write a story set at the turn of the millennium at midnight on January 1, 2000.

176.   Write a story set in a forest.

177.   Write a story set in the middle of a Christmas town called Santa Claus.

178.   Write a story set on a beach.

179.   Write a story set in a cozy cabin in the woods.

180.   Write a story set on a luxury yacht.

181.   Write a story set in a toy factory.

182.   Write a story set on a balcony overlooking a lake.

183.   Write a story set in Paris.

184.   Write a story about a traveller who boards a ship and docks in a strange land.

185.   Write a story about vacationing on the island of Jamaica.

186.   Write a blog post on tips to save money for a vacation.

187.   Write a blog post on what to look for when buying a new smartphone.

188.   Write a story or dialogue about time travelling to the Victorian era. What gadgets would you bring from the modern era to show some of your new friends from that era?

189.   Write a blog post about how to make friends.

190.   Write a blog post about fun activities to do in the summer.

191.   Write a dialogue between parents arguing about where to have their next family vacation.

192.   Write a conversation between a person interviewing for a new job and the interviewer.

193.   Write a dialogue between a reporter and a
       Hollywood star on the red carpet of a movie
       premier.

194.   Write a scene involving a press conference
       and a celebrity clearing up rumors.

195.   Write a paragraph about your day off work
       or school. What did you do?

196.   Write a paragraph about your work process
       as a writer.

197.   Write a journal entry about your daily
       rituals.

198.   Write a journal entry about everything you
       ate today or yesterday.

199.   Write a journal entry about everyone you
       texted or spoke to today or yesterday.

200.   Write a journal entry about the conversation
       you would have with your favorite celebrity or
       person you admire.

*"Every secret of a writer's soul, every experience
of his life, every quality of his mind,
is written large in his works."*
— Virginia Woolf

Prompts 201-250

Finish the sentence, then write a paragraph.

201.   He cherished the memory of…

202.   "You would never guess what I…"

203.   She slid the phone back into her purse when…

204.   A warm feeling…

205.   "Promise me, you'll…"

206.   Who are you?

207.   He eyed her with…

208.   I will always…

209.   Are you sure about…

210.   She grinned sheepishly when…

211.   Her eyes captured her surroundings.…

212.   A flicker of apprehension coursed through her…

213.   Something about him…

214.   Could she do this? Could she really…

215.   Her hand shook as she reached for the…

216.   Guilt flooded through him…

217.   Euphoria washed over her…

218.   He longed to…

219.   Reaching out to him meant…

220.   He took a step forward into the…

221.   She prepped herself for …

222.   She looked up; her eyes widened with shock when…

223.   She stood back, surprised…

224.   She stood at the top of the hill…

225.   She braced herself for the…

226.   She was going to tell him…

227.   "Penny for your thoughts."

228.   "It's complicated," she said. "I…"

229.   There's more to…

230.   I always carry a…

231.   The last thing on my mind at night…

232.   The first thing I think about in the morning
        when I rise…

233.   I am devoted to…

234.   My loyalty for…

235.   "Come in. Quick!" she shouted…

236.   "I need a job. Like yesterday…"

237.   "Can you do this for me?"

238.   "How can I be of service?" she asked.

239.   "You'll never guess who I ran into…"

240.   "This is so embarrassing…"

241.   "Oops! I can't believe I just…"

242.   "I just bought a…"

243.   "Oh, no. Did I just one-click…"

244.   "Oh, no. I sent my photo to the wrong
contact…"

245.   "If you didn't get my text, then who…"

246.   "I just received a text message from…"

247.   "He's outside my window, singing…"

248.   "It's beautiful. He gave me a…"

249.   He swooped in and…

250.   He swept me off my feet and…

*"There is no greater agony than bearing
an untold story inside you."*
— Maya Angelou

Prompts 251 – 300

251.   A cat is on the ledge. What would you do to help her.

252.   He wants to marry his arch enemy. What would you say to him?

253.   You just found out your now late enemy requested that you eulogize them. What would you say?

254.   You see a crack on the sidewalk. What do you do?

255.   You accidentally spilled salt on the table and patrons in the restaurant are watching you. Describe how you feel.

256.   Write a poem about a job ad for an animal trainer.

257.   Write a blog post on tips on how to train a dog.

258.   Your cat can suddenly speak to you. What are his first words?

259.   Write a story about a person who has glossophobia, fear of public speaking.

260.   Write a story about a person who has ergophobia, fear of work.

261.   Write a story about a person who has kakorrhaphiophobia, fear of failure.

262.   Write a story about a person who has peniaphobia, fear of being broke.

263.   Write a story about a person who has been caught in the rain and has astraphobia, fear of thunderstorms.

264.   Write a story about the day in the life of a cab driver.

265.   Write a story about the day in the life of an art gallery owner.

266.   Write a story about the day in the life of a
beauty salon owner.

267.   Numbers, numbers, numbers. Write a story
about a day in the life of your accountant.

268.   Write a story about the day in the life of an
actress.

269.   Write a story about the day in the life of an
allergist.

270.   Write a story about the day in the life of a
rock star.

271.   Write a story about the day in the life of a
bodyguard.

272.   Write a story about the day in the life of a
coach.

273.   Write a story about the day in the life of an
aerobics instructor.

274.   Write a story about the day in the life of an inventor of robots.

275.   Write a story about the day in the life of an advertising executive.

276.   Write a story about the day in the life of an attorney.

277.   Write a story about the day in the life of a grocery clerk.

278.   Write a story about the day in the life of a baker.

279.   Write a story about the day in the life of a librarian.

280.   Write a story about the day in the life of a bookstore owner.

281.   Write a story about the day in the life of a bank teller.

282.   Write a story about the day in the life of a chef.

283.   Write a story about the day in the life of a dating service app developer.

284.   He's waiting for the answer. The answer is…

285.   She glanced out the window and gasped when she saw…

286.   A smile curved her lips when…

287.   He asked her to run away with him to…

288.   He had to be married by the end of the week because…

289.   Yes! It's finally here…

290.   Her shoes…

291.   His eyes reminded her of…

292.   Ocean-blue eyes gazed into hers and…

293.   Rich mahogany-colored eyes penetrated hers and…

294.   Her heart turned over in her chest when…

295.   When she opened the door, her jaw fell open…

296.   She slid into her nightgown and…

297.   You know when you're in trouble when…

298.   Truth is always stranger than…

299.   When things get good…

300.   I'm in control of…

"I can shake off everything as I write, my sorrows disappear, my courage is reborn."
— Anne Frank

Prompts 301- 350

You have five seconds to write anything about the following words…

301.   Cat

302.   Morning

303.   Your job

304.   Your favorite hobby

305.   Running

306.   Exercise

307.   Dessert

308.   Planes

309.   Forrest

310.	Grass

311.	Plants

312.	Flowers

313.	Heater

314.	Sun

315.	Moon

316.	Earth

317.	Movies

318.	Your favorite TV shows

319.	Your favorite gadget

320.	Your favorite food

321.   Your favorite place to relax

322.   Your favorite book to read

323.   Your favorite place to vacation

324.   Ocean

325.   Tranquility

326.   Calm

327.   Relaxing

328.   Surreal

329.   Mesmerized

330.   Rapture

331.   Energized

332.   Vivacious

333.   Invigorated

334.   Elated

335.   Giddy with joy

336.   Radiant

337.   Cheerful

338.   Beach

339.   Garden

340.   Park

341.   Forest

342.   Bay

343.   Dock

344.   Lake

345.   Cabin

346.   Camping

347.   Excursion

348.   Trip

349.   Leadership

350.   Staycation

Prompts 351- 400

351.   It's Saturday morning. What do you enjoy
doing?

352.   Describe what you'd be doing on your
dream day off.

353.   Write a poem about the word "shout."

354.   Write a poem about the word "shriek."

355.   Write a poem about the word "frantic."

356.   Write a poem about the word "joy."

357.   Write a poem about the word
"accomplishment."

358.   Write a poem about the word "forever."

359.   Write a poem about the word "garden."

360.   Write a poem about the word "love."

361.   Write a poem about a cold winter's night.

362.   Write a poem about reading on the beach.

363.   Write a poem about the warm sand grains in your sandals.

364.   Write a poem about the taste of your favorite dessert on your tongue.

365.   Write a poem about the word "incredulous."

366.   Write a story about a superhero who has just lost his powers for the day.

367.   Write a dialogue between a dog and a cat who just found out they are now housemates.

368.   Write a letter to your town about how you feel about living there.

369.   Write a poem about your favorite month of
the year.

370.   Write a poem about your favorite luxury
beverage.

371.   Write a poem about the word "cynical."

372.   Write a poem about the word "perceptive."

373.   Write a poem about the word "insightful."

374.   Write a poem about the word
"accomplished."

375.   Write a poem about the word "dream."

376.   Write a poem about the word "shrewd."

377.   Write a poem about the word "evergreen."

378.   Write a poem about the words "my cell
phone."

379.   Write a poem about the word "artful."

380.   Write a poem about the word "cautious."

381.   Write a poem about the word "savvy."

382.   Write a poem about the word "clever."

383.   Write a poem about the word "versatile."

384.   Write a poem about the word "deep."

385.   Write a poem about the word "complicated."

386.   Write a poem about the word "mesmerized."

387.   Write a poem about the word "euphoria."

388.   Write a poem about the word "boring."

389.   Write a poem about the word "humor."

390.   Write a poem about the acronym "LOL (laugh out loud)."

391.   Write a poem about the word "endless."

392.   Write a poem about the word "obsessed."

393.   Write a poem about the word "quirky."

394.   Write a poem about the word "manipulative."

395.   Write a poem about the word "ocean."

396.   Write a poem about the word "sunset."

397.   Write a poem about the word "sunshine."

398.   Write a poem about the word "storm."

399.   Write a poem about the word "weather."

400.   Write a poem about the words "in love."

*'If you write one story, it may be bad; if you write a
hundred, you have the odds in your favor.'*
~ Edgar Rice Burroughs

Prompts 401- 450

401.   Name your favorite childhood hobby.

402.   Name a time when you got caught in a little lie.

403.   Write a poem about your day.

404.   Write a poem about your evening.

405.   Write a poem about what you did at work today.

406.   Write a poem about your neighbor.

407.   Write a story about running a mile.

408.   Write a story about getting your own way.

409.   Write a story about winning the lottery six times!

410.   Write a story about climbing a mountain.

411.   Write a story about learning how to fish for the first time.

412.   Write a story about your very first pet.

413.   Write a story about the day in the life of a cartoonist.

414.   Write a story about the day in the life of a female car wash attendant.

415.   Write a story about the day in the life of a caterer for weddings.

416.   Write a story about the day in the life of a coast guard.

417.   Write a story about the day in the life of a stand-up comedian.

418.   Write a story about the day in the life of a dog groomer.

419.   Write a story about the day in the life of a novelist.

420.   Write a story about the day in the life of driver's ed instructor.

421.   Write a story about the day in the life of a marriage counselor.

422.   Write a story about the day in the life of a dental hygienist.

423.   Write a story about the day in the life of a paramedic.

424.   Write a story about the day in the life of a nurse.

425.   Write a story about the day in the life of pilot of a small private plane for the super-rich.

426. Write a story about the day in the life of a radio DJ.

427. Write a story about the day in the life of a YouTuber.

428. Write a story about the day in the life of an amateur photographer.

429. Write a story about the day in the life of a pet sitter.

430. Write a story about the day in the life of a fitness or Yoga instructor.

431. Write a story about the day in the life of a painter.

432. Write a story about the day in the life of a yacht captain.

433. Write a story about the day in the life of a cruise ship staff member.

434.	Write a story about the day in the life of an airline flight attendant.

435.	Write a story about the day in the life of a salesperson at a smartphone store.

436.	Write a story about taking a stroll in the park on a sunny afternoon.

437.	Write a story about a visit to the barber shop or hair salon.

438.	Write a story about a conversation at a nail salon.

439.	Write a story about forging ahead.

440.	Write a story about choosing the right name for your pet.

441.	Write a story about a doll.

442.	Write a story about a toy car.

443.   Write a story about a fly on the wall—from the perspective of the fly.

444.   Write a story about visiting a ranch and riding a horse.

445.   Write a story about a long road-trip.

446.   Write a story about a night school class.

447.   Write a story about science class.

448.   Write a story about rushing to school on a rainy day.

449.   Write a story about eating at a popular restaurant with your friends.

450.   Write a story about going on a shopping spree with your friends.

Prompts 451-500

You have ten seconds to list anything that comes to mind when you see the following words:

451. Ostentatious

452. Dreamy

453. Sparkling blue water

454. Warm sandy beach

455. Cloudless blue sky

456. Sipping pina colada on a beach

457. Ocean waves

458. Quiet stream

459. Warm island breeze

460.   Koi pond

461.   Water fountain

462.   Relaxing on a ranch

463.   Sitting on the front porch

464.   Stars blanketing the night sky

465.   Snowflakes falling

466.   Ocean view

467.   Panoramic view of the skyline

468.   Edible gold

469.   Christmas present

470.   Pudding

471.   Eggnog

472.   Festive decorations

473.   Bright city lights

474.   Fur baby

475.   Cuddly

476.   Hot chocolate with whipped cream

477.   Custard-filled donut

478.   Crispy fries

479.   Chicken wings

480.   Sleigh ride

481.   Crunchy snack

482.   Warm milk

483.   Wintery night

484.   Blizzard

485.   Cuddle by the fireplace

486.   Relaxing on the couch

487.   Warm glow of a candlelight

488.   Flames flickering in the fireplace

489.   Daydreaming of that special person

490.   Spending a quiet evening inside

491.   Marble

492.   Best friend for life

493.   Barbecue

494.   Mansion

495.   Garden house

496.   A day at the zoo

497.   Locked in at the museum

498.   ATM

499.   Online

500.   Riding into the distance

***

Thank you for taking this journey with *500 Writing Prompts*. I hope you found this book helpful. Remember to read and enjoy the written word. The more you read, the more ideas flow, the more you exercise your creativity and imagination, the more you become one with the written word.

For more information on other books in the series, you can send S. A. M. Richards a message at pageturningstories@gmail.com